W9-CCY-215

TED WILLIAMS